DK READERS

STAR WARS

THE CLONE WARS

Anakin In Action!

Written by Simon Beecroft

DK

A group of gunships fly through
the sky.
Each gunship carries soldiers
and Jedi generals.
The gunships are flying very fast.
They are on a dangerous mission.

Gunships
Gunships carry
soldiers into
battle.

Some important people
are inside the gunships.

One of them wears
a robe with a hood.
He is called Anakin.
He is a Jedi Knight.

Jedi Knights
Jedi Knights are brave
people with special powers.

A soldier stands next to Anakin.
This soldier is Captain Rex.
Captain Rex wears a special
helmet over his face.
His body is protected by armor.

Another Jedi is traveling in
the gunship with Anakin.
Her name is Ahsoka.
Ahsoka is still learning her Jedi
powers. Anakin is her teacher.

Ahsoka has special
white patterns on her red skin.
She also has long head tails.

Alien Jedi
Ahsoka is an alien.
Aliens are different
from humans.
They come from
other worlds.

Anakin, Ahsoka, and the clone
soldiers land close to a big castle.

They are going to rescue a young
creature called Rotta.
Rotta is a prisoner inside the castle.

Anakin is ready with his lightsaber!

Clone soldiers
Clones are humans who all look and behave the same way.

Enemy droids stand at the top of the castle wall. They see Anakin and the others land.

Spider droids have red eyes and walk on four mechanical legs. They start firing their big guns.

Battle droids also start firing.
Watch out Anakin!

Droid soldiers
Battle droids are not
human soldiers. They
are machine soldiers.

13

Anakin, Ahsoka, and the clone
soldiers reach the castle wall.
It is so high they can hardly see
the top.
Captain Rex fires ropes out of his
blaster. The ropes hook onto the
top of the wall.

The Jedi and the soldiers all grab hold of the ropes and start climbing up. Anakin goes first and Ahsoka follows close behind. Clone soldiers in big tanks also start climbing the wall.

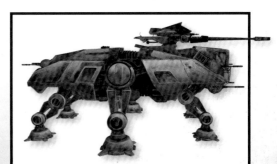

Clone tanks
These big tanks walk on six powerful legs. They can also climb walls.

Anakin has almost reached the top of the castle wall when battle droids on flying machines start to attack. Anakin thinks quickly.

He jumps onto one of the machines as it flies past.

STAPs
These flying machines are called STAPs. They have blaster cannons on the front.

Anakin kicks the droid off his
flying machine.
Now he attacks the other droids!

After a lot of fighting, Anakin
and Ahsoka reach the top of
the castle wall.
They enter the castle.
The castle is cold and dark.

Baby Hutt
Rotta is a creature called
a Hutt. Ahsoka carries
him in a backpack.

Anakin and Ahsoka sneak
along the creepy corridors.
Soon, they are able to find Rotta.
He is just a baby.
They must rescue Rotta quickly.
They must leave the castle quickly.

Too late! The droids
have blocked the exit.
Someone is with them.
This person looks dangerous.
She holds a lightsaber with
a red blade.

Her name is Ventress.
She has special powers like a Jedi.
Anakin, Ahsoka, and Captain Rex
run back inside the castle
and lock the door.

Ventress breaks down the door to the castle. She goes inside to look for Anakin and Ahsoka.

In a dark room, Ventress finds Anakin and Ahsoka.
Anakin has nowhere to run.
He lights his blue lightsaber.
Ventress and Anakin fight each other with their lightsabers.
Clash!

Jedi enemy
Ventress uses a lightsaber like a Jedi. But she is not a Jedi. She is a deadly enemy of the Jedi.

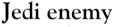

22

23

Ahsoka is looking after Rotta.
She is carrying him on her back.
But she sees that Anakin needs
her help.

Ahsoka jumps into the fight.
Ventress growls and
attacks Ahsoka.
Now all three of them
are fighting!

Ahsoka tries to find a way out of the dark room. She opens a heavy door. Big mistake!

A huge monstrous shape comes out of the shadows.
It is a rancor monster.

The rancor has sharp teeth and claws. It roars and attacks!

Rancors
Rancors are dangerous monsters with big heads and sharp claws and teeth.

Anakin and Ventress jump
onto the rancor's back
and continue fighting.
The rancor is confused.
It can no longer see Anakin
and Ventress.

Then the rancor
spots Ahsoka
and Rotta.

It moves toward them, as Anakin
and Ventress fight on its back.
Ahsoka stabs the rancor's foot.

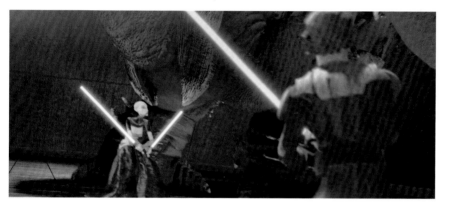

It howls in pain and falls right
on top of Ventress. Squish!

Anakin and Ahsoka think that the rancor has crushed Ventress. They escape from the castle with Rotta.

But after they have gone, there is a noise: vzzz!

It is a lightsaber being turned on.
Ventress is still alive!

Outside, Anakin tells Ahsoka
she was a great Jedi today.
A gunship arrives to take
them away. They are off
on another adventure!

Clone Wars Facts

Anakin Skywalker uses a lightsaber with a glowing blue blade.

Ahsoka uses a lightsaber with a green blade.

Ventress's lightsabers have red blades.

Captain Rex goes on missions with Anakin.

Rotta has thick, oily skin and orange eyes.